PALEO COOKING
Bootcamp
for Busy People

KATIE FRENCH

RESULTS + TESTIMONIALS

"I took Katie's Paleo Cooking Bootcamp (her first class!) and it was a great experience. I was already eating Paleo (maybe 80% of the time), but I was overwhelmed by how time consuming many of the online recipes were to make. Katie provided very simple recipes and food preparation techniques that helped me become more efficient in the kitchen as well as look forward to the few hours it takes to prepare a week's worth of home cooked and HEALTHY meals! I'm now 100% Paleo and continue to make a lot of the meals that Katie taught us in the Bootcamp. My favorite is the Collard Greens Wrap, Broccoli Salad, Bacon Wrapped Meatballs, and Paleo Muffins...although actually, it is all delicious!" (S.W., Nurse)

"I took Katie's Paleo Cooking Bootcamp, which was a life-changing experience. I knew about the Paleo philosophy - but much of it seemed 'too complicated' to use on a daily basis. Now thanks to Katie, I am able to manage my sugar-craving and addiction to processed foods. I love her simple, organized approach to menu-planning and food preparation. There is never a shortage of food, nor am I hungry during the week. My goals for weight loss and a healthier lifestyle are now possible as my food cravings have been replaced with real nutrition and higher energy." (A.H., Executive)

"I joined Katie's Paleo Cooking Boot-camp to kickstart 2015 and add to my workout routine. During her Cooking Bootcamp, I lost 8 pounds, and saw an improvement in both my energy and mood. I love the Paleo Breakfast Muffin recipe and cooking in an industrial kitchen! The ease of the recipes cannot be overstated. It really is possible to cook for the week in a couple of hours!" (D.R., Attorney)

"I took the Paleo Cooking Bootcamp and LOVED it! Prepping all of our food for a whole week in 2 hours was pretty impressive, and a lot easier than I expected. Katie introduced us to so many new, healthy alternatives to add to our everyday lifestyle. I would say the most valuable thing from this class was learning how different things affect my overall health and well-being. I had no idea how much of an affect sugar, dairy, bread, etc. had on me until I removed them for a full month. That is a life-changer!" (K.F., Sales)

Library of Congress Cataloging-in-Publication Data

Names: French, Katie, author.
Title: Paleo cooking bootcamp for busy people / by Katie French.
Description: Oxnard, CA : Primal Blueprint Publishing, [2017] | Includes
  index.
Identifiers: LCCN 2016056445 (print) | LCCN 2016057616 (ebook) | ISBN
  9781939563347 (hardcover) | ISBN 9781939563347 (epub)
Subjects: LCSH: Natural foods. | Nutrition. | Cooking. | LCGFT: Cookbooks.
Classification: LCC TX369 .F74 2017 (print) | LCC TX369 (ebook) | DDC
  641.3/02-- dc23
LC record available at https://lccn.loc.gov/2016056445

Project Manager: Caroline De Vita
Editor: Tracy Kearns
Design & Layout: Katie French and Caroline De Vita
Cover Design: Janée Meadows
Index and Proofreading: Tim Tate
Photography: Cherie Azzopardi and Austin Daniels
Stock and Farmers' Market Photos: Todd Sanchioni
Photo on page 10 ©iStock: Lauri Patterson

Publisher: Primal Blueprint Publishing, 1641 S. Rose Ave., Oxnard, CA 93033
For information on quantity discounts, please call 888-774-6259 or 310-317-4414, email: info@primalblueprintpublishing.com, or visit PrimalBlueprintPublishing.com.

TABLE OF CONTENTS

ABOUT THE AUTHOR

From Litigation Attorney to Health Coach – My Call to Action

Just a few short years ago, I was finishing up my fifth year as a litigation attorney, after graduating from the prestigious University of California, Hastings College of the Law in San Francisco. I always knew I wanted to become an attorney, announcing it to everyone in my life from the young age of eight. I single-mindedly pursued the goal, graduating college in three years, and becoming an attorney by the age of twenty-four.

But there was a moment when I vowed to give it all up. It happened during an 18-minute TED Talk presentation by chef, Jamie Oliver, discussing the health crisis in America. Chef Oliver revealed that for the first time in history, our children will have shorter lifespans than their parents, and that we now have three generations of Americans who have never learned how to cook.

I was utterly stunned by this. I could not fathom the idea that there are three generations of American families who have never learned how to cook so that all of their meals are pre-made, processed or from restaurants, including fast food restaurants. Even as an insanely busy, overly stressed-out attorney, I managed to cook almost 100% of my meals and snacks. If I could do it, than anyone could do it, I thought. And in that moment, my call to action was as clear as anything I've ever felt in my life.

So after 5 years, I wound up a successful law practice, and obtained a degree as a health coach. I started seeing clients for nutritional counseling, including some of the attorneys with whom I had previously worked. The focus of my practice was to help my clients streamline the process of meal planning, grocery shopping, and cooking for the week.

I began coaching my clients on the strategies and methods that had worked for me as an attorney: each weekend I'd write up a meal plan, go to the Farmer's Market and grocery store and then spend about two to three hours in my kitchen cooking as much food as I could manage. I became very efficient at this process (because I didn't have a lot of time to spare!) and eventually I had several meal plans made up of easy, healthy and satisfying recipes which created enough meals and snacks for the entire week.

Many of my clients became very interested in this "make-ahead" method of cooking, and so I started offering private cooking lessons, teaching my clients how to cook all of their meals and snacks for the week in under two hours. My clients loved this service, and the benefits were undeniable.

I wanted to teach this concept on a larger scale, so I started a cooking class series called *Paleo Cooking Bootcamp*. I rented space at a commercial kitchen just south of San Francisco, and got in contact with some local organic farmers to supply the groceries. My clients would show up and cook with me for 2 hours each week, on Sundays. I would arrange for all the groceries to be delivered prior to the class, and each student would have his/her own cooking station, equipped with a complete set of kitchen supplies and groceries. I would instruct the class, step-by-step, through the recipes, and by the end of the two-hour class, each student would leave with all the food they had prepared, which was enough breakfast, lunch, dinner and snack options for the entire week.

My *Paleo Cooking Bootcamp* class was awarded the prestigious "Best of SF" designation by *San Francisco Magazine*, as well as the "As Fresh As It Gets" award by the San Mateo County/Silicon Valley Convention and Visitors Bureau.

I am proud to offer this unique cookbook that provides a systematized and stress-free approach to the process of meal planning, grocery shopping and cooking each week. Cooking ahead for the week makes it simple to stay on track with healthy eating, which in turn contributes to better energy so that we can keep up with and enjoy our busy lives.

Here's my advice to you: in order to accomplish healthy eating, you must become intentional about the process of meal planning, grocery shopping, and cooking each week. (I am sorry, but there's just no other way!) I am excited and honored to give you this shortcut to the process: *Paleo Cooking Bootcamp for Busy People*!

In Good Health,
Katie

HOW TO USE

Paleo Cooking Bootcamp was the name of my award-winning cooking class in San Francisco, where my clients would cook with me for two hours, and take home all of the food they prepared. The recipes we prepared during each two-hour class created enough breakfast, lunch, dinner and snack options for the entire week!

This book contains a month's worth of menus from my Paleo Cooking Bootcamp class. For each week, there is a Grocery List and a Cooking Order List (detailing the order to cook everything), along with step-by-step instructions and photos for all the recipes. All of the recipes for each week's menu can be prepared in two to three hours at home, freeing up your time to do more of the things that you love to do! At the end of the cookbook are checklists for each week's Grocery List and Cooking Order List. They are "working copies" of these lists that can be copied or pulled out and used when you are grocery shopping and prepping/preparing your meals for the week.

By following this cookbook you are going to eliminate hours of time each week that you would otherwise spend planning out your meals, collecting recipes, preparing a grocery list, and cooking recipes that may not turn out well or that may be too time consuming to accomplish in one cooking session.

These weekly cooking plans can be prepared in just a few hours once a week. The ingredients for each cooking plan will cost between $100 to $150 per week, as long as you already have the staple pantry ingredients like spices and oils, otherwise expect that you will pay more in the beginning to build up your pantry.

These recipes are easy enough for the average home cook, but they are also delicious and satisfying so that eating this way can become a lifestyle and not just a diet!

THIS BOOK

RECOMMENDATIONS

INGREDIENTS:

PRODUCE

In order to label produce as "organic", farmers must grow it using natural fertilizers (manure or compost), without the use of pesticides or herbicides. On the other hand, farmers growing conventional produce may use synthetic or chemical fertilizers, herbicides (for weed control) and pesticides.

Residues from the chemical or synthetic fertilizers, herbicides and pesticides remain on (and in) the produce we eat, at levels that would shock most people. I encourage you to do your own research, but I think you will find that the scientifically-documented dangers of at least some of these chemicals are not worth the risk to your health, nor that of your loved ones.

Most of us have accumulated some chemical residue in our bodies simply from living around them all our lives. Research suggests that some of this unnatural, human-caused chemical toxicity (and let's remember, not all chemicals are toxic and some degrade rather quickly) may be attributed to health issues ranging from headaches, birth defects, and suppressed immune systems. Some studies indicate that exposure to some pesticides (even at low doses) can increase the risk of certain cancers, such as leukemia, lymphoma, brain tumors, breast cancer and prostate cancer. Finally, children and fetuses are deemed most vulnerable to pesticide exposure due to their still-developing immune systems, bodies, and brains. Chemical exposure may even play a role in some developmental delays, behavioral disorders, autism, immune and motor dysfunction. This is why going organic to reduce the synthetic chemical load in our environment and in ourselves makes so much sense.

"Going organic" may be more expensive. Buying organic produce from your local farmers' market, or as part of a local CSA (community-supported agriculture) program, could make it more cost effective or at least comparable to the price of conventional produce from the grocery store. Nonetheless, when one calculates the health risks posed for both the environment as well as for humans from so much unnatural chemical exposure, the price of "going organic" seems cheap by comparison.

Don't forget that produce is most nutritious when it is harvested at its peak maturity. Asparagus picked yesterday and sold today at your farmer's market, doesn't just taste better than asparagus sold at the grocery store. It is also better for you because once fruits and vegetables are picked, the nutrients start to degrade. Asparagus sold in the grocery store may take up to two weeks from harvest to processing and transportation to your grocery cart, refrigerator and dinner plate. If enhanced flavor and nutrition aren't good enough reasons to check out your local farmers' market, think about how great it is to support your community and neighboring farmers.

Finally, consider starting your own garden! This is an immensely rewarding experience, and if you're a parent, there is no better way to get your kids interested in healthy eating! (I've never heard of a child who helped grow veggies in a garden who didn't love cooking those veggies and eating them!) Fresh herbs and spices are an added benefit to cooking many of the recipes in this cookbook.

Growing herbs and spices are a great way to experiment with gardening. As with fruits and vegetables, herbs and spices not labeled "organic" in the grocery store may be treated with chemicals, therefore it is better to spring for the chemical-free brands. Buying in bulk can significantly reduce cost or better yet, you can try growing some of your own.

ANIMAL PRODUCTS

You are what you eat, right? Well, the same is true of the animals you eat. What animals ingest, whether it is food, environmental chemicals or antibiotics, as well as the amount of fresh air, sunlight and exercise they get directly impacts the quality of their meat, which in turn directly impacts your own health.

Meat from a healthy animal is highly nutritious and even anti-inflammatory, whereas meat from an unhealthy animal can cause toxins to accumulate in your body, and may even cause inflammation.

Here is what you need to know about the health of the animals you consume:

- **Beef:** Cows are only supposed to eat grass. If they eat anything else, like corn or grains, they often get sick and end up on antibiotics. Some are already sick or dying when they reach the slaughter-house. So buying "grass-fed" meat is the only way to ensure that the beef you eat is healthy for you.
- **Chicken:** Chickens are meant to roam free outdoors eating grass, seeds and bugs! Chickens that are caged up all day without the opportunity for exercise and sunlight, also have a tendency to sicken and require antibiotics. The same requirement goes for the eggs that are laid by those chickens. (Unfortunately labeling for chicken and eggs can be misleading: "cage-free" does not necessarily mean they get to run around in the sunlight and eat bugs. It may just mean they are crammed inside a barn all day, without cages.) The best way to ensure healthy chicken meat and eggs is to purchase " pasture-raised" products.
- **Other meats:** Choose meat products with the label "pasture-raised" to ensure that the animals were raised under healthier conditions, which translates to healthier meat for your body.
- **Fish:** Wild-caught fish will always be healthier, because they are in their natural habitat, receiving the nutrition and exercise that is natural to their species. In addition, farm raised fish may have a higher exposure to toxins and pollutants.

Note: the label "organic" for meat merely denotes that the animals' feed is organic, and/or not genetically modified. "Organically" fed animals are usually treated by natural means (rather than with antibiotics) if they get sick, and are typically given "some" access to the outdoors. These living conditions are clearly superior to that of animals not fed naturally or organically. Conventionally farmed animals often receive growth hormones for faster, bigger development, as well as non-organic, GMO feed and antibiotics (and other medicines) to prevent disease. Nor do conventionally grown animals typically get access to the outdoors. Be aware, however, that the label "organic" does not ensure that an animal ate a diet natural to its species, nor that it receives adequate sunlight and exercise for optimal health. Look also for the designation "pasture-raised".

If you are concerned about the cost of buying higher-quality meat, research whether you can buy pasture-raised, organic meat directly from a local rancher at a lower cost. I've worked with many families and individuals who have purchased entire animals or done an animal share with others to keep costs down. Also, local butchers tend to have a lower mark-up cost than grocery stores, and they usually know a lot more about the sourcing and quality of the meat they sell.

COOKING SUPPLIES

COOKWARE:

In my work as a cooking coach, I have seen the inside of a lot of kitchens and I've found that, unfortunately, most people still use plastic cookware and food storage containers. Plastic breaks down over time (especially when heated) leeching harmful chemicals into the food you eat, chemicals that have been linked to cancer, compromised brain and heart health.

It is worth the extra investment to buy higher quality, safer materials to protect the health of you and your loved ones. I highly recommend replacing all of your plastic cookware, including utensils, measuring cups, measuring spoons, mixing bowls, cutting boards, and food storage containers with the following recommendations:

- **<u>Stainless Steel</u>** for utensils and mixing bowls: Stainless steel cookware is very tough; it does not chip or rust, and is scratch resistant. It also does not leach its metallic properties into food.
- **<u>Bamboo</u>** for cutting boards and utensils: Bamboo is a highly renewable resource that can be economically and ethically sourced, so using bamboo is both sustainable and eco-friendly. For cutting boards, bamboo is also the best, healthiest material, because unlike plastic or wood, cutting on a bamboo board does not create cuts, which can allow moisture, food particles and bacteria to accumulate. Bamboo is dense enough to resist knife scarring and also naturally resists water penetration, which prevents bacteria from accumulating.
- **<u>Glass</u>** for measuring cups, food storage containers, baking dishes and mixing bowls: Glass cookware and food storage containers do not leach chemicals into your food, even when heated. Glass food storage containers, like, mason jars, can also be very inexpensive when you buy them in bulk!

UTENSIL RECOMMENDATIONS

Food processor Recommend Cuisinart 11-cup capacity; and the following blades: S-blade, slice blade, and shred blade

Cutting board Recommend bamboo or other eco-friendly material and two if cooking with another

Silicon muffin pans Two 12-cup pans

Mixing bowls Recommend stainless steel in small, medium and large

Santoku knife

Kitchen shears Recommend KitchenAid

Measuring spoons Recommend stainless steel utensils measuring 1 and ½ tablespoons; ⅛ , ¼ , ½ , and 1 teaspoon

Measuring cups Recommend stainless steel measuring ¼ , ⅓ , ½ , and 1 cup

Microplane for grating

Garlic press

Spiralizer

Can opener

Masher

Whisk

Silicon spatula

Peeler

Digital meat thermometer

Wooden, straight-edged spatula

Slotted spoon Wooden or metal

Non-stick pan Recommend 12-inch Scan Pan or any enameled cast-iron pan

Oven-safe skillet 12-inch

Dutch oven with lid Recommend 7-quart Scan Pan, or any enameled cast-iron pot

Rimmed baking sheets Two 12x17-inch sheets

Baking rack One to fit onto a 12x17-inch baking sheet

Glass baking dish Oblong, 3-quart with silicon lid

Glass measuring cup with spout 2-cup capacity

Glass pie plate

Oven mitts

Wide-mouth quart-size mason jars with lids (five)

Pint-size mason jar with lid (one)

WEEK #1
GROCERY SHOPPING TIPS

Many of my clients like to break up the weekly grocery shopping and cooking session into two separate days, so consider doing your groceries on Saturday and carving out time on Sunday for your cooking session.

A few ways to save time:

1. Once you get home from the grocery store, group the ingredients for each recipe together in the fridge and in your pantry.

2. When you get home from the grocery store, pre-wash, chop and dice your veggies for that week's recipes. For example, peel and slice your carrots for the Ragu; prepare your butternut squash, and slice your mushrooms and then store them in the fridge for the next day's cooking session. The most time-consuming part of cooking is often the vegetable prep, so save time by preparing your veggies the night before your cooking session.

3. Some grocery stores sell ready-made, spiralized veggies, for those recipes that call for them (ie; the Ragu recipe). Otherwise, you can purchase an inexpensive spiralizer at any kitchen or home goods store.

4. To store your greens, use a knife or kitchen shears to poke several small holes in both sides of a large Ziploc bag, and store the greens in the bag in the fridge. This gives the greens just enough oxygen to stay fresher longer. Do this as soon as you get your groceries home, to ensure optimal freshness.

5. Buy your half pound of mushrooms pre-sliced to save prep-time this week.

6. Buy minced fresh garlic from your grocer to save time.

7. Buy mild Italian sausage in bulk versus in casings, when possible.

8. Select among the several brands of "Paleo Bacon" or "Sugar-Free Bacon" when possible.

9. *Primal Kitchen* sells its own brand of Avocado Oil. You will be using a lot of avocado oil over the next month! The reason? It's loaded with good fat, and cooks at a higher heat temperature than the other oils. Our three favorite Paleo-approved oils are avocado oil (for high temperature cooking); unrefined coconut oil (for lower temperature cooking, under 350 degrees, as the oil breaks down at higher temps, becoming a potential toxin), and olive oil (which has such a low smoke point that it should never be used for cooking, and should be used instead at room temperature in salad dressings and sauces). All other cooking oils are to be avoided as they produce inflammation in most people.

10. Always look for sprouted nuts and seeds, when possible, as they are easier for our bodies to digest.

11. Nuts: raw is preferred, dry roasted is okay, but avoid any nuts with added (inflammatory) oils or other ingredients.

12. Almond butter: make sure that there are no ingredients in the almond butter other than almonds or salt.
13. Himalayan sea salt: for all my recipes I recommend the use of Himalayan sea salt. Some sea salt can be contaminated with toxins and pollutants, but Himalayan sea salt is considered a more pure source.
14. Cacao nibs: buy 100% cacao, without added sugar, soy or dairy. Enjoy the flavor of chocolate and get the antioxidant benefits as well.
15. Paleo condiments: pick up some *Primal Kitchen* Mayonnaise at your local grocer for your Collard Greens Sandwich Wraps! It's Paleo-approved, healthy, convenient and delicious!
16. Lemon juice: buy a small bottle of 100% lemon juice to save time.
17. Spices: check your pantry to make sure you have the basics on hand, as well as what is listed on each week's grocery list. I recommend buying organic spices, for the same reason as your produce - pesticides may be used if the product is not specifically labeled organic. Also, spices expire, so it might be time to replace them. Check the labels of the vanilla extract and baking soda to make sure they are free of additives.

WEEK #1 MENU ITEMS FOR EACH DAY

Breakfast:
▶ 1-2 Paleo Energy Muffins
▶ 1 piece of Breakfast Casserole

Snacks:
▶ Raw Veggie Snack Bag and Paleo Hummus
▶ Raw Veggie Snack Bag
▶ 1-2 Paleo Energy Muffins
▶ 1 slice of Breakfast Casserole

Lunch/dinner
▶ Collard Greens Sandwich Wrap
▶ Collard Greens Sandwich Wrap and Raw Veggie Snack Bag
▶ Collard Greens Sandwich Wrap and Raw Veggie Snack Bag and Paleo Hummus
▶ Paleo Winter Ragu (1 cup/225g per serving)
▶ Paleo Winter Ragu (1 cup/225g as topping for spaghetti squash or spiralized veggies)

WEEK #2
GROCERY SHOPPING TIPS

1. Check Grocery Shopping Tips from Week 1 as they will apply for each week.
2. Make the spice rub for the Carnitas and marinate the meat in the fridge the night before your cooking session.
3. The day of your cooking session, put the carnitas in the slow cooker first thing in the morning, as they take eight hours to cook.
4. Use unrefined coconut oil because refined coconut oil is often chemically treated.
5. Make sure to buy almond flour, rather than almond meal.
6. Buy pre-chopped walnuts to save time.
7. Choose ingredients such as Dijon mustard and balsamic vinegar without additives.
8. Make sure you have five quart-size mason jars for the Mason Jar Salads.
9. Order *Otto's Naturals* Cassava Flour online for next week's recipes!

WEEK #2 MENU ITEMS FOR EACH DAY

Breakfast
- 1-2 Paleo Banana Nut Muffins
- 1-2 Paleo Egg Muffins

Snacks
- 1-2 Paleo Banana Nut Muffins
- 1-2 Paleo Egg Muffins
- Mason Jar Salad

Lunch/dinner
- Carnitas with Fajita Veggies
- Roasted Chicken and Mason Jar Salad
- Roasted Chicken and Fajita Veggies
- Carnitas and Mason Jar Salad

WEEK #3
GROCERY SHOPPING TIPS

1. Hopefully, you already ordered *Otto's Naturals* Cassava Flour last week!
2. Once you bring your groceries home, make the marinade for the Paleo Honey Garlic Flank Steak and marinate the meat in the fridge overnight.
3. Be sure to buy coconut flakes, rather than shredded coconut.
4. Look for raw, wildflower honey from your region as a natural antihistamine.
5. *Primal Kitchen* Chipotle Lime Mayonnaise (available at your local grocery store) is a must-have ingredient for your fish tacos!

WEEK #3 MENU ITEMS FOR EACH DAY

Breakfast
- ▶ 1 piece of Paleo Frittata
- ▶ Paleo Granola (½ cup/78g)
- ▶ Cauliflower Fried Rice (1 cup/325g)

Snack
- ▶ 1 piece of Paleo Frittata
- ▶ Paleo Granola (½ cup/78g)
- ▶ Cauliflower Fried Rice (1 cup/325g)
- ▶ Cauliflower Buffalo Wings (1 cup/325g)

Lunch/dinner
- ▶ 1 piece of Honey Garlic Flank Steak and Cauliflower Fried Rice (1 cup/325g)
- ▶ 1 piece of Honey Garlic Flank Steak and Cauliflower Buffalo Wings (1 cup/325g)
- ▶ Paleo Fish Tacos (2)
- ▶ Paleo Fish Tacos (2) and Cauliflower Buffalo Wings (1 cup/325g)

WEEK #4
GROCERY SHOPPING TIPS

1. Butter – definitely go for grass-fed butter, it's worth the extra money!
2. Buy ingredients without extra additives.

WEEK #4 MENU ITEMS FOR EACH DAY

Breakfast
- ▶ 1 slice of Paleo Quiche
- ▶ 1-2 Paleo Pumpkin Muffins
- ▶ 2-3 Bacon-Wrapped Green Beans

Snacks
- ▶ 1 slice of Paleo Quiche
- ▶ 1-2 Paleo Pumpkin Muffins
- ▶ 2-3 Bacon-Wrapped Green Beans

Lunch/dinner
- ▶ Spiced Ground Beef and Mexican Cauli-Rice (1 cup/325g)
- ▶ Spiced Ground Beef Tacos
- ▶ Spiced Ground Beef Tacos and Mexican Cauli-Rice (1 cup/325g)
- ▶ Tuna Salad and 2-3 Bacon-Wrapped Green Beans

WEEK #1

MEALS + SNACKS

▶ Breakfast Casserole

▶ Paleo Energy Muffins

▶ Paleo Winter Ragu with Roasted Spaghetti Squash (or Veggie Noodles)

▶ Paleo Collard Greens Sandwich Wraps with Paleo Hummus + Raw Veggie Snack Bags

GROCERY LIST
WEEK #1

Recommendations: buy organic and locally grown produce; buy organic, pasture-raised meat, poultry and eggs; and buy wild-caught fish, whenever possible.

PRODUCE

- Spaghetti squash (2-3 pounds/1-1.36kg, or if not available, 2 yams, spiralized)
- Yams (2)
- Baby spinach (5 ounces/142g)
- Collard greens (12 large leaves)
- Any veggies you like on your sandwiches (ie; 2-3 tomatoes, or 1 red onion, etc.)
- Yellow onion (1)
- Carrots (9)
- Cherry tomatoes (1 pint)
- Cucumbers (1-2; for Raw Veggie Snack Bags)
- Butternut squash (1 small; or if not available, 2 yams)
- Garlic cloves (2 cloves and 2 tablespoons, minced)
- Mushrooms (½ pound/227g, sliced)
- Cauliflower (1 head)

MEAT + POULTRY + FISH + EGGS

- 1½ dozen eggs
- 1 pound/454g mild Italian pork sausage
- 12 slices of lunch meat (if using 2 slices per sandwich wrap)
- 2 packages of bacon
- 1 pound/454g ground beef
- 1 pound/454g ground pork

NUTS + SEEDS + OILS

- Avocado oil (¼ cup/56ml and 2 tablespoons, plus more to coat baking dish)
- Extra virgin olive oil (EVOO) (½ cup/112ml)
- Tahini (⅓ cup/79ml)
- Almond butter (½ cup/113g - the only ingredients should be almonds, and salt or no salt)
- *Go Raw* Organic, Sprouted Sunflower Seeds (½ cup/58g)
- Unsweetened, shredded coconut (½ cup/50g)

SPICES

- Vanilla extract (1 teaspoon)
- Cinnamon (1 teaspoon)
- Baking soda (¼ teaspoon)
- Himalayan sea salt (1¼ teaspoon, plus more to taste)
- Cumin (½ teaspoon)

CANNED + JARRED + PACKAGED GOODS

- Maple syrup (½ cup/175g)
- Cacao nibs (½ cup/58g)
- Any *Paleo* condiments you like on your sandwiches (*Primal Kitchen* Mayo, mustard, Paleo pickles, etc.)
- Tomato paste (6-ounce/180ml can)
- *Cucina Antica* Garlic Marinara sauce (one 32-ounce/904g jar)
- Lemon juice (⅓ cup/79ml)

COOKING SUPPLIES

- Parchment paper muffin liners (one dozen)
- Aluminum foil
- Parchment paper
- Sandwich-size plastic bags (5)

COOKING ORDER WEEK #1:

1. Preheat the oven to 350°F (180°C).
2. Make <u>Paleo Energy Muffins</u>.
3. Turn up the oven to 400°F (200°C).
4. Make <u>Roasted Spaghetti Squash</u>.
5. Make <u>Breakfast Casserole</u>.
6. Put the casserole in the oven with the <u>Roasted Spaghetti Squash</u>.
7. Make <u>Paleo Winter Ragu</u>. (Simmer for 1 hour.)
8. Turn up the oven to 425°F (220°C).
9. Make the bacon for <u>Paleo Collard Greens Sandwich Wraps</u>.
10. Roast cauliflower for <u>Paleo Hummus</u>.
11. Put the cauliflower in the oven with the bacon.
12. Make <u>Paleo Collard Greens Sandwich Wraps</u> (*recommendation*: do not pre-make all sandwich wraps; it's best to make them throughout the week, on the day of or night before).
13. Make <u>Raw Veggie Snack Bags</u>.
14. Make <u>Paleo Hummus</u>.

COOKING TIPS

Start by preheating your oven for the first recipe each week.

Follow the cooking order list as you move from recipe to recipe. I included a cooking order list for each week for efficiency. You will start with the lowest temperature dishes in the oven first, turning up the heat as you go, and in some cases I recommend putting two dishes in the oven at once, to cook together and save time.

PALEO ENERGY MUFFINS

Hands-On Time: 10 minutes
Cook Time: 15 minutes
Makes: 12 muffins

INGREDIENTS

½ cup (113g) almond butter (the only ingredients should be almonds and salt or no salt)

1 egg

½ cup (175g) maple syrup

½ cup (50g) unsweetened, shredded coconut

½ cup (58g) cacao nibs

½ cup (58g) sprouted sunflower seeds (try: *Go Raw* Organic brand)

1 teaspoon vanilla extract

1 teaspoon cinnamon

¼ teaspoon baking soda

¼ teaspoon Himalayan sea salt

1 dozen parchment paper muffin liners

METHOD

1. Preheat the oven to 350°F (180°C).
2. Combine all ingredients in a large mixing bowl.
3. Line a muffin tin with 12 parchment paper muffin liners.
4. Scoop 1 tablespoon of batter into your hands, form a ball, and place each ball into a muffin cup. (You may need to wet your hands to avoid having the batter stick to them.) If you have extra batter, divide it evenly between the muffin cups.
5. Bake these muffins for 7 minutes, then turn the pan 180 degrees and bake for another 7 minutes.

NOTES

- *This is a great one-bowl recipe: You can add all your ingredients to one mixing bowl and stir everything together to make your batter. It is also easy to double the recipe and the muffins are freezable. If you use a silicon muffin pan, parchment paper muffin liners will not be necessary.*
- ***Egg-free option:*** *for an egg-free option, use 1 banana, mashed, in place of egg.*
- ***Nut-free option:*** *for a nut-free option, use sunflower butter in place of almond butter.*

Hands-On Time: 5 minutes
Cook Time: 30-45 minutes
Makes: 4-6 servings

ROASTED SPAGHETTI SQUASH

INGREDIENTS

2-3 pounds (1-1.36kg) spaghetti squash

Filtered water

METHOD

1. Preheat your oven to 400°F (200°C).
2. Slice the ends off the squash. Then cut the squash lengthwise.
3. Use a spoon to scrape out the seeds and strings from inside the squash.
4. Place the squash, cut-side halves down, in a casserole dish or rimmed baking sheet.
5. Pour a little filtered water into the dish, just enough to cover the bottom.
6. Cook the squash for 30-45 minutes.
7. The squash is ready when you can easily pierce a fork through the flesh all the way to the peel.
8. Use a fork to gently scrape the squash flesh from the peel, from top to bottom.
9. Eat spaghetti squash (in lieu of pasta noodles) with your Paleo Ragu.

NOTES

If the squash is too hard to cut through safely, try microwaving it for a few minutes to soften. But always pierce the skin (as with potatoes) before cooking.

If spaghetti squash is not available, serve the Paleo Ragu over sautéed spiralized yams or zucchini!

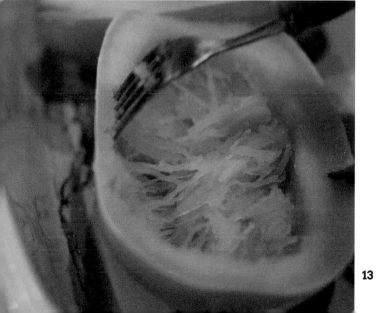
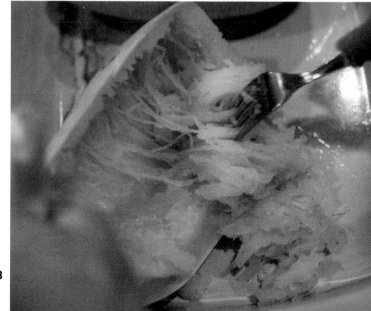

BREAKFAST CASSEROLE

Hands-On Time: 15 minutes   **Cook Time**: 35-40 minutes   **Makes**: 8-10 servings

INGREDIENTS

1 pound (454g) mild Italian pork sausage

2 yams

17 eggs

5 ounces (142ml) baby spinach

1-2 tablespoons of avocado oil
(plus more to coat baking dish)

Himalayan sea salt, to taste

METHOD

1. Preheat the oven to 400°F (200°C).

2. Heat 1-2 tablespoons of avocado oil in a fry pan over medium to medium-high heat. Crumble the sausage into the pan, breaking up lumps. If your sausage is in casings, remove from the casings using a knife or kitchen shears.

3. When the sausage is almost fully cooked, add the spinach to the pan, and salt, to taste. Cook until the sausage is browned and the spinach is wilted.

4. Peel and shred your yams, using the shred blade of your food processor.

5. Coat the sides and bottom of your 3-quart casserole dish with avocado oil.

6. Add the shredded yams to the bottom of the greased baking dish so that it forms a bottom layer for the casserole.

7. Spread the meat and spinach mixture evenly over the shredded yams.

8. Whisk your raw eggs in a mixing bowl. Add salt to the eggs, to taste.

9. Pour your whisked eggs into the baking dish, covering the yams, meat and spinach.

10. Bake for 35-40 minutes.

NOTES

Try using a casserole dish with a lid, to make storing in the fridge easier. This is a "template recipe" which means you can substitute another type of meat for the sausage, or add any other veggies you might prefer! This dish is also freezable.

Hands-On Time: 25 minutes **Cook Time**: 1½ hours **Makes**: A lot!

PALEO WINTER RAGU

INGREDIENTS

2-4 tablespoons avocado oil

1 yellow onion

1 pound (454g) ground beef

1 pound (454g) ground pork

1 package bacon

6 garlic cloves (or 2 tablespoons, minced)

4 large carrots (peeled and sliced into thin discs)

1 small butternut squash (peeled and cubed; if not available, then 2 yams, peeled and cubed)

½ pound (227g) mushrooms (sliced thinly)

1 6-ounce (180ml) can tomato paste

1 32-ounce (904g) jar *Cucina Antica* Garlic Marinara sauce (available at Whole Foods)

Himalayan sea salt, to taste

METHOD

1. In a large wok or skillet, heat 1-2 tablespoons of avocado oil over medium to medium-high heat.

2. Dice your onion, add the diced onion to the fry pan, and cook until the onion is translucent.

3. Add the ground beef and pork to the fry pan, and season with salt. Stir in the fresh minced garlic. Cook until the meat is browned. Set aside.

4. Heat a large Dutch oven over medium to medium-high heat. Using your kitchen shears, cut the slices of bacon into your Dutch oven, cutting the pieces of bacon crosswise into ¼ to ½-inch pieces. Cook your bacon fully (to your preference), and remove from the Dutch oven using a slotted spoon, so that the bacon fat remains in the pot.

5. Peel your carrots, and set aside.

6. To prepare your butternut squash: cut off the top of the squash, and cut the squash in half, crosswise. Cut each half of the squash in half again, lengthwise. Scoop out any seeds and strands with a spoon. Peel the skin off, and cut into long pieces that will fit through the top of your food processor.

7. Slice your carrots and butternut squash using the slice blade on your food processor.

8. Add your sliced carrots and butternut squash to the bacon fat in your Dutch oven and cook until tender (add the lid to cook faster).

9. Slice your mushrooms using the slice blade on your food processor. Set aside.

10. When you've cooked the carrots and butternut squash to your preferred tenderness, add the cooked beef, pork and bacon bits to the Dutch oven. Then add in your diced mushrooms, tomato paste, and marinara sauce, stirring everything together.

11. Add salt, to taste.

12. Simmer for 1 hour.

NOTES

This ragu is loaded with veggies, so you can eat it by itself, or serve it over spaghetti squash or a spiralized vegetable like squash. This recipe makes a lot and is also freezable.

PALEO COLLARD GREENS SANDWICH WRAPS

Hands-On Time: 20 minutes
Cook Time: 20-25 minutes (Paleo Bacon)
Makes: 6 sandwiches

INGREDIENTS

12 large leaves of collard greens

Your favorite Paleo condiments and veggies: *Primal Kitchen* Mayo, mustard, Paleo pickles, tomatoes, red onion, etc.

12 slices of lunch meat (if using 2 slices per sandwich wrap)

1 package bacon

Aluminum foil

Parchment paper

METHOD

1. Preheat the oven to 425°F (220°C).

2. Cover a large rimmed baking sheet (12 x 17 inches) with parchment paper. Place a rack on top of the baking sheet. Lay the bacon pieces on the rack, making sure that they do not overlap. Cook the bacon for 20-25 minutes. Save the bacon fat in a jar and store in the fridge to use as a cooking oil!

3. To assemble the sandwich wraps, first lay down a piece of aluminum foil that is slightly bigger than the circumference of two collard green leaves. Lay the same size piece of parchment paper on top of the aluminum foil.

4. Place two leaves of collard greens onto the parchment paper, overlapping to create one long leaf, with the veiny side of each leaf facing up. Cut off the excess stem from the bottom of the leaf with a knife.

5. Start with your Paleo condiments – spread them onto the leaf with a butter knife.

6. Next, put two pieces of lunchmeat on top of the condiments.

7. Put two pieces of cooked bacon on top of the lunchmeat. Store the rest of the cooked bacon in the fridge to save for your next sandwich.

8. Add any additional veggies on top of the bacon (for example: Paleo pickle slices, tomato slices, sliced red onion, etc.).

9. Fold in both ends of the leaves. Then roll up the leaves lengthwise like a burrito. Lastly, roll your sandwich wrap in parchment paper and then in aluminum foil.

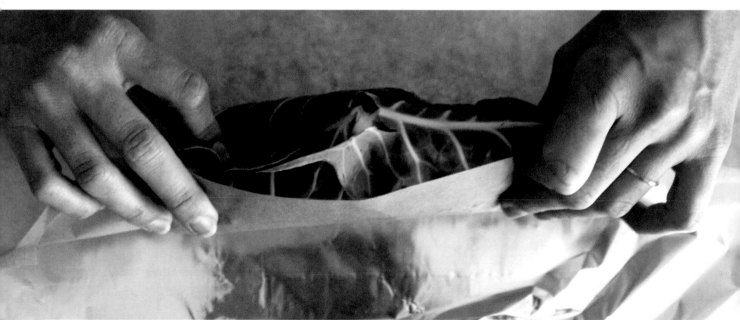

NOTES

Prepare these with any ingredients that you would normally put on your favorite sandwich. **Recommendation:** *do not pre-make all sandwich wraps; it's best to make them fresh each day, or the night before.*

PALEO HUMMUS + RAW VEGGIES

Hands-On Time: 25 minutes **Cook Time**: 30 minutes **Makes**: 5 servings

INGREDIENTS

Paleo Hummus

1 head of cauliflower
(cut into florets; about 2 cups/300g)

⅓ cup (79ml) tahini

⅓ cup (79ml) lemon juice

2 garlic cloves (peeled)

½ teaspoon cumin

1 teaspoon Himalayan sea salt

½ cup (112ml) extra virgin olive oil
(EVOO)

Parchment paper

Raw Veggie Snack Bags

5 carrots

1 pint cherry tomatoes

1-2 cucumbers

5 sandwich-size plastic bags

METHOD

Paleo Hummus

1. Preheat the oven to 400°F (200°C).

2. To prepare your cauliflower, remove the green leaves/stems, and cut out the core with your knife. Cut off any excess stems, and cut the cauliflower into florets of equal size.

3. Cover a 12 x 17-inch rimmed baking sheet with parchment paper.

4. Put the florets on the parchment paper and bake for 30 minutes.

5. While the cauliflower is roasting, combine your tahini and lemon juice in a food processor. Scrape down the sides of the food processor canister, and process again.

6. Add your garlic cloves, cumin, salt, and EVOO to the food processor, and process to combine. Scrape down the sides of the food processor canister, and process again.

7. Add the roasted cauliflower florets to the food processor in 1-2 batches and process to combine.

Raw Veggie Snack Bags

1. Peel your carrots, and cut into matchsticks.

2. Cut your cucumbers into matchsticks.

3. Divide equal portions of the veggies (matchstick carrots, cucumbers, and whole tomatoes) into 5 storage containers or Ziploc bags and store in the fridge!

NOTES

Paleo Hummus: Remember that legumes are not Paleo-approved, so this recipe swaps the garbanzo beans for cauliflower – yay extra veggies!

Raw Veggie Snack Bags: Several clients claim they make these raw veggie snack bags every single week as ready-to-go snacks for when they're in a hurry. Substitute or add any veggies you like.

MEALS + SNACKS

▶ Paleo Banana Nut Muffins

▶ Paleo Egg Muffins

▶ Carnitas with Fajita Veggies

▶ Roasted Chicken with Mason Jar Salads + Simple Vinaigrette

WEEK #2

GROCERY LIST
WEEK #2

Recommendations: buy organic and locally grown produce; buy organic, pasture-raised meat, poultry and eggs and wild-caught fish whenever possible.

PRODUCE

- Cherry tomatoes (1 pint)
- Carrots (6)
- Cucumbers (2)
- Green onions (1 bunch)
- Radishes (1 bunch)
- Beet (1)
- Spinach (5 ounces/142g) or Romaine lettuce (1 bunch)
- Garlic cloves (1 teaspoon, minced)
- Sun-dried tomatoes (2 ounces/57g)
- Leek (1)
- Mushrooms (1 pound/454g)
- Bananas (4, very ripe)
- Bell peppers (4, any color)
- Yellow onion (1)

MEAT + POULTRY + FISH + EGGS

- 3 pounds/1.36kg pork shoulder/butt (ask the butcher to cut into two 1½-pound/680g pieces)
- 3 pounds/1.36kg boneless, chicken thighs (or any other preferred type of chicken)
- 1 pound/454g mild Italian pork sausage
- 14 eggs

NUTS + SEEDS + OILS

- Extra virgin olive oil (EVOO) (½ cup/112ml)
- Avocado oil (¾ cup/177ml)
- Unrefined coconut oil (¼ cup/56ml)
- Almond flour (2 cups/280g)
- Walnuts (½ cup/65g, chopped)

SPICES

- Smoked paprika (6 tablespoons, plus more to taste)
- Garlic cloves (1 teaspoon, minced)
- Garlic granules, to taste
- Garlic powder (2 tablespoons)
- Ground mustard (2 tablespoons, plus more to taste)
- Himalayan sea salt (3 tablespoons and ¾ teaspoon, plus more to taste)
- Ground black pepper (¼ teaspoon)
- Vanilla extract (1 teaspoon)
- Baking soda (½ teaspoon)

CANNED + JARRED + PACKAGED GOODS

- Dijon mustard (1 teaspoon)
- Balsamic vinegar (3 tablespoons)
- Maple syrup (¼ cup/56ml)

COOKING SUPPLIES

- Parchment paper
- Parchment paper muffin liners (2 dozen)

COOKING ORDER

WEEK #2:

1. **The night before**: Make the spice rub for the Carnitas and marinate the meat in the fridge **overnight**.

2. **The morning of**: Put the Carnitas in the slow cooker as soon as you wake up in the morning, since they will need to cook for 8 hours on low.

3. Preheat the oven to 350˚F (180˚C).

4. Make the Paleo Banana Nut Muffins.

5. Turn up the oven to 375˚F (190˚C).

6. Make the Paleo Egg Muffins.

7. Turn up the oven to 400˚F (200˚C).

8. Make Roasted Chicken.

9. Make Fajita Veggies (Just pre-cut the veggies, and cook up one serving; store the rest of the pre-cut veggies in the fridge and cook up a serving the day of or the night before).

10. Make Mason Jar Salads.

11. Make Simple Vinaigrette.

Hands-On Time: 10 minutes
Cook Time: 8 hours (in slow cooker)
Makes: 4-6 servings

CARNITAS

INGREDIENTS

3 pounds (1.36kg) pork shoulder/butt
(cut into two 1½-pound/680g pieces)

6 tablespoons smoked paprika

2 tablespoons garlic powder

2 tablespoons ground mustard

3 tablespoons Himalayan sea salt

37

NOTES

This recipe requires a slow cooker and the meat needs to marinate in the fridge overnight.

METHOD

The night before: Prepare the spice rub by combining the smoked paprika, garlic powder, dry mustard and sea salt in a bowl. Rub the spice rub all over the pieces of pork and place each piece in Ziploc bags or food storage containers to **marinate** in the **fridge overnight**.

If you have extra spice rub left over, store it in your pantry in a sealed mason jar for next time.

1. When you're ready to cook the pork, place the marinated pieces in your slow cooker on low for 8 hours.
2. After 8 hours, shred the pork apart using 2 forks, and stir all of the shredded pieces with the flavored juices from cooking.

PALEO BANANA NUT MUFFINS

Hands-On Time: 15 minutes
Cook Time: 20-25 minutes
Makes: 12-15 muffins

INGREDIENTS

4 bananas (very ripe)

¼ cup (56ml) maple syrup

2 eggs

¼ cup (56ml) unrefined coconut oil (melted)

1 teaspoon vanilla extract

2 cups (280g) almond flour

½ teaspoon baking soda

½ teaspoon Himalayan sea salt

½ cup (65g) walnuts (chopped)

1 dozen parchment paper muffin liners

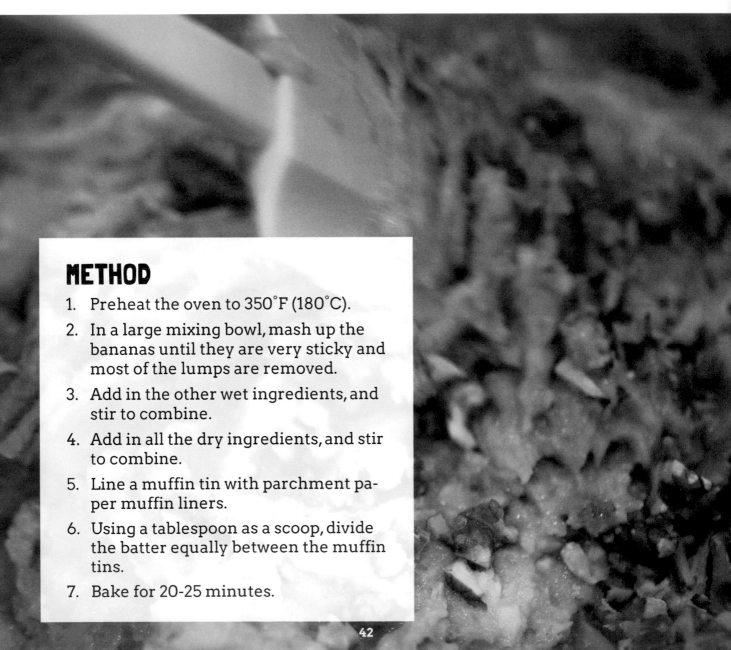

METHOD

1. Preheat the oven to 350°F (180°C).

2. In a large mixing bowl, mash up the bananas until they are very sticky and most of the lumps are removed.

3. Add in the other wet ingredients, and stir to combine.

4. Add in all the dry ingredients, and stir to combine.

5. Line a muffin tin with parchment paper muffin liners.

6. Using a tablespoon as a scoop, divide the batter equally between the muffin tins.

7. Bake for 20-25 minutes.

NOTES

This is a one-bowl recipe, like the Paleo Energy Muffins, but remember to mash the bananas up first in the bottom of the bowl before you add the rest of the ingredients. Freezable!

PALEO EGG MUFFINS

Hands-On Time: 20 minutes
Cook Time: 30-35 minutes
Makes: 12 muffins

INGREDIENTS

1 pound (454g) mild Italian pork sausage

1 dozen eggs

2 ounces (56g) sun-dried tomatoes

1 leek

½ pound (227g) mushrooms

1-2 tablespoons avocado oil

Himalayan sea salt, to taste

1 dozen parchment paper muffin liners

METHOD

1. Preheat the oven to 375°F. (190°C).

2. Heat 1-2 tablespoons of avocado oil in a fry pan over medium to medium-high heat. Crumble the sausage into the pan, breaking up lumps. If your sausage is in casings, remove it from the casings using a knife or kitchen shears. Cook until the sausage is browned.

3. Dice your leeks and add to a mixing bowl.

4. Using your kitchen shears, chop your sun-dried tomatoes into small pieces and add to the mixing bowl with the diced leeks.

5. Dice your mushrooms using the S-blade on your food processor, and add the diced mushrooms to the bowl with the leeks and sun-dried tomatoes.

6. Using your hands or a spoon, fully mix together the veggies.

7. Line a muffin tin with parchment paper muffin liners.

8. Add the veggie mixture to the bottom of the muffin cups, filling up each cup about one third full. (If you have extra veggies, store in the fridge and sauté another time with eggs for a delicious scramble!)

9. Using a spoon, transfer all the cooked sausage equally into the muffin cups, on top of the veggie mixture.

10. Whisk the raw eggs in a mixing bowl. Add salt, to taste, to the eggs.

11. Transfer the whisked, raw eggs into a measuring cup with a spout and pour the eggs over the top of the sausage and veggies, until each muffin cup is almost full with the eggs.

12. Bake for 30-35 minutes.

NOTES
Great breakfast for on-the-go.
Tastes great hot or cold and freezable.

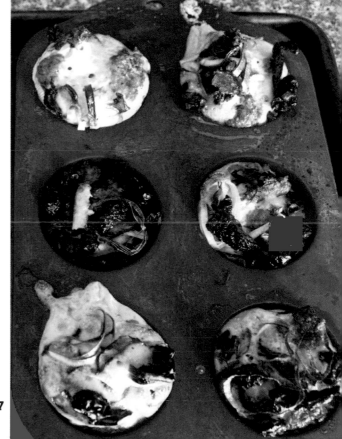

ROASTED

CHICKEN

INGREDIENTS

3 pounds (1.4kg) boneless, chicken thighs (or other preferred part of chicken)

Himalayan sea salt, to taste

Smoked paprika, to taste

Garlic granules, to taste

Ground mustard, to taste

Parchment paper

METHOD

1. Preheat the oven to 400°F (200°C).
2. Cover a 12 x 17-inch baking sheet with parchment paper.
3. Place the chicken on the parchment paper, smooth side facing down.
4. Season the chicken generously with salt, smoked paprika, garlic and ground mustard.
5. Flip the chicken and season the other side.
6. Bake for 30-35 minutes.
7. Check the chicken with a meat thermometer – the internal temperature should be 165°F (74°C).

FAJITA VEGGIES

Hands-On Time: 20 minutes
Cook Time: 5-7 minutes
Makes: 5 servings

INGREDIENTS

1-2 tablespoons avocado oil (per serving)

4 carrots

½ pound (227g) mushrooms

4 bell peppers (any color)

1 yellow onion (chopped)

Himalayan sea salt, to taste

52

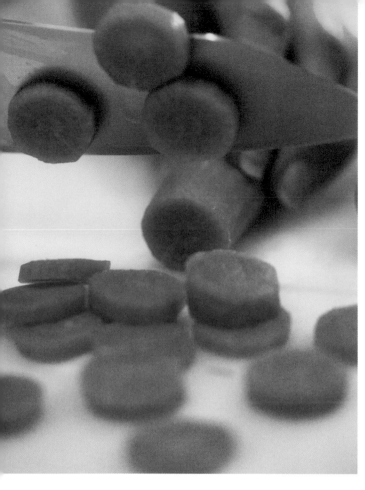

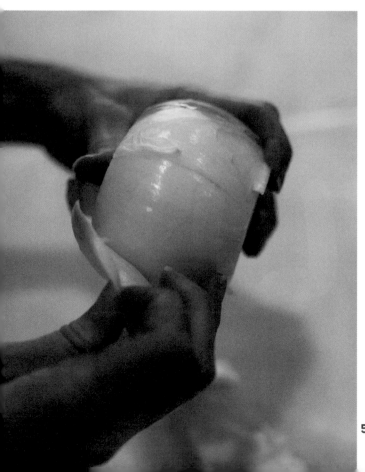

METHOD

1. Peel your carrots, and slice thinly. Add to a large mixing bowl.
2. Slice your mushrooms, and add to your mixing bowl.
3. Cut your bell pepper into long pieces ("julienned"), removing all seeds and ribbing. Add to your mixing bowl.
4. Dice your onion, and separate the onion pieces by hand. Add to your mixing bowl.
5. Using your hands, mix all of the veggies together.
6. Store these pre-cut veggies in the fridge until you are ready to cook up a serving!
7. To cook: Heat up enough avocado oil to coat the bottom of a fry pan over high heat.
8. Place 1-2 cups (or handfuls) of the veggies in the pan, add salt to taste, and sauté for 5-7 minutes, until the veggies are cooked as you like them.

NOTES

Pre-cut the veggies, and store them in the fridge, to cook up a serving each day or the night before.

MASON JAR SALADS + SIMPLE VINAIGRETTE

Hands-On Time: 25 minutes **Makes**: 5 salads

INGREDIENTS

Mason Jar Salads
1 pint cherry tomatoes

1-2 cucumbers

1 bunch green onions

2 carrots

1 bunch radishes

1 beet

5 ounces (142g) spinach or Romaine lettuce (1 bunch)

Simple Vinaigrette
1 teaspoon Dijon mustard

1 teaspoon minced garlic clove (using a garlic press)

3 tablespoons balsamic vinegar

¼ teaspoon Himalayan sea salt

¼ teaspoon ground black pepper

½ cup (112ml) extra virgin olive oil (EVOO)

METHOD

1. Start with 5 quart-size (32 liquid ounces or 946 ml each) wide-mouth mason jars.

2. Prepare salads like an assembly line, packing each ingredient into each jar in the order listed below.

3. Put your whole cherry tomatoes in the bottom of each of the five mason jars.

4. Chop your cucumbers and distribute them evenly between all five mason jars.

5. Chop your green onions and distribute them evenly between all five mason jars.

6. Peel your carrots, slice thinly and add them to your mason jars.

7. Remove both ends of your radishes, chop them, and add them next to your mason jars.

8. Put down a piece of parchment paper on your cutting board, peel your beets, chop them, and add them to your mason jars.

9. Fill the mason jars the rest of the way with your baby spinach or romaine lettuce.

10. Put the lids on all five jars and store in the fridge!

11. <u>Simple Vinaigrette:</u> Add all ingredients to a small mason jar, put on the lid and shake to combine. Store dressing in the sealed jar in the fridge. Add to your salad when you are ready to eat!

59

59

MEALS + SNACKS

▶ Paleo Granola

▶ Paleo Frittata

▶ Honey Garlic Flank Steak with Veggie-Fried Cauliflower Rice

▶ Paleo Fish Tacos with Cauliflower Buffalo Wings

WEEK #3

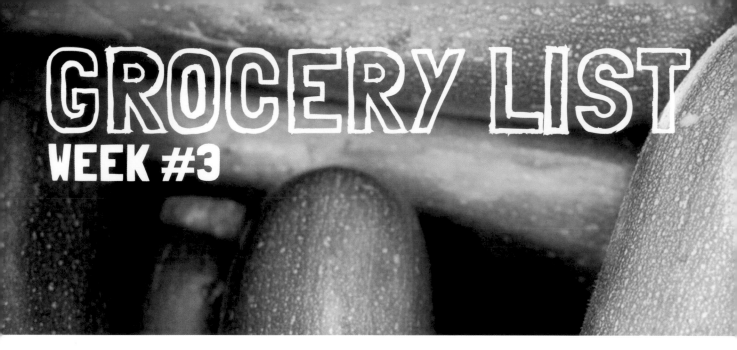

GROCERY LIST
WEEK #3

Recommendations: buy organic and locally grown produce; buy organic, pasture-raised meat, poultry and eggs; and buy wild-caught fish, whenever possible.

PRODUCE

- Garlic cloves (4 cloves plus 1 tablespoon, minced)
- Cauliflower (2 large heads or 4 small)
- Carrots (4)
- Zucchini (1 large or 2 small)
- Mushrooms (½ pound/227g)
- Fresh ginger (1-inch square piece)
- Yam (1)
- Asparagus (1 bunch)
- Cherry tomatoes (1 pint)
- Green onions (1 bunch)
- Any veggies you like on your Paleo Fish Tacos (pico de gallo or other favorite salsa; guacamole; cilantro; diced onion; shredded cabbage; lime juice, etc.)

MEAT + POULTRY + FISH + EGGS

- 1½ pounds/681g flank steak (ask the butcher to cut the steak into six 4-ounce/113.5g pieces)
- 1 package bacon
- 18 eggs
- 1 pound/454g mild Italian, pork sausage
- 1 pound of a white flaky fish (skin removed) such as cod, mahi mahi, or tilapia

NUTS + SEEDS + OILS

- Avocado oil (1⅓ cup and 4 teaspoons/ 335ml, plus more to fry the steaks)
- Coconut aminos (⅓ cup plus ¼ cup/ 135ml; recommend *Coconut Secrets*)
- Coconut vinegar (1 tablespoon; recommend *Coconut Secrets*)

- Unsweetened coconut flakes (1 cup/115g)
- Unrefined/extra virgin coconut oil (¼ cup/50g)
- Almond flour (1 cup/115g)
- Raw almonds (1 cup/115g)
- Raw cashews (1 cup/115g)
- Raw pumpkin seeds (1 cup/115g)
- Raw sunflower seeds (1 cup/115g)

SPICES

- Himalayan sea salt (2¼ teaspoons, plus more to taste)
- Smoked paprika (1 teaspoon)
- Garlic powder (1 teaspoon, plus more to taste)
- Vanilla extract (1 teaspoon)
- Cumin, to taste
- Chili powder, to taste
- Paprika, to taste
- Onion powder, to taste

CANNED + JARRED + PACKAGED GOODS

- Apple cider vinegar (1 tablespoon)
- Hot sauce (1 teaspoon; only whole, natural ingredients and spices)
- Raw honey (½ cup/88g)
- Cacao nibs (1 cup/115g)
- *Primal Kitchen* Chipotle Lime Mayo as a condiment for your Paleo Fish Tacos

COOKING SUPPLIES

- Parchment paper

ONLINE

- *Otto's Naturals* Cassava Flour (1¾ cup/214g)

COOKING ORDER
WEEK #3:

1. **The night before** make the marinade for the <u>Paleo Honey Garlic Flank Steak</u> and **marinate the meat** in the fridge *overnight*.

2. Preheat the oven to 350°F (180°C).

3. Make the <u>Paleo Granola</u>.

4. Make the <u>Paleo Frittata</u>.

5. Make the <u>Veggie-Fried Cauliflower Rice</u>.

6. Turn up the oven to 375°F (190°C).

7. Make the fish for the <u>Paleo Fish Tacos</u>.

8. Turn up the oven to 425°F (220°C).

9. Make <u>Cauliflower Buffalo Wings</u>.

10. Make the tortillas for the <u>Paleo Fish Tacos</u>.

11. Make <u>Honey Garlic Flank Steak</u>.

NOTES

*Marinate the steak in the fridge **overnight**.*

HONEY GARLIC FLANK STEAK

Hands-On Time: 10 minutes **Cook Time**: 4-8 minutes **Makes**: 6 servings

INGREDIENTS

1½ pounds (681g) flank steak, cut into six 4-ounce (113.5g) pieces

⅓ cup (75ml) avocado oil (plus more to fry the steak)

4 garlic cloves (minced with garlic press)

1 tablespoon apple cider vinegar

⅓ cup (75ml) coconut aminos (recommend *Coconut Secrets)*

¼ cup (88g) raw honey

¼ teaspoon Himalayan sea salt

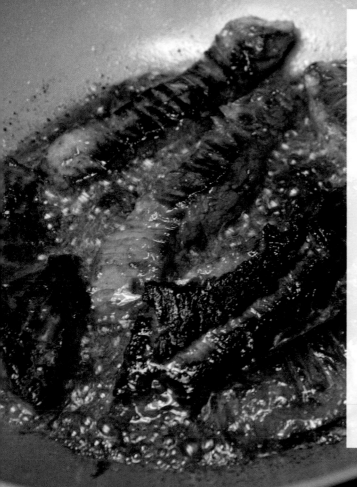

METHOD

1. Place the steak slices into a large Ziploc bag.

2. Prepare the marinade by combining the avocado oil, minced garlic, apple cider vinegar, coconut aminos, honey, and salt. Whisk together and pour into the Ziploc bag, submerging the steak in the marinade.

3. ***Let the steak marinate in the fridge overnight***.

4. When you're ready to cook the steak, heat up enough oil to coat the bottom of a fry pan over high heat.

5. Lay the steak pieces down into the pan and sear each side for 2 to 4 minutes, depending on the thickness of the meat (do not overcook or the meat will become very tough!).

PALEO GRANOLA

Hands-On Time: 15 minutes
Cook Time: 20 minutes
Makes: 10-12 servings

INGREDIENTS

1 cup (115g) raw almonds

1 cup (115g) raw cashews

1 cup (115g) raw pumpkin seeds

1 cup (115g) raw sunflower seeds

1 cup (115g) unsweetened coconut flakes

1 cup (115g) cacao nibs

¼ cup (50g), softened unrefined extra virgin coconut oil

½ cup (175g) raw honey

1 teaspoon vanilla extract

1 teaspoon Himalayan sea salt

Parchment paper

METHOD

1. Preheat the oven to 350°F (180°C).
2. Combine all ingredients in a large mixing bowl, making sure to coat everything in the honey.
3. Line the bottom of a 3-quart casserole dish with parchment paper.
4. Transfer the granola mixture onto the parchment paper and spread out the mixture evenly to form a thin layer on the bottom of the baking dish.
5. Bake for 20 minutes.
6. Allow to cool for about 30 minutes or until hardened.

PALEO FRITTATA

Hands-On Time: 20 minutes
Cook Time: 45 minutes
Makes: 8-10 servings

NOTES

You need an oven-safe fry pan for this recipe.

INGREDIENTS

1 pound (454g) Italian pork sausage

1 dozen eggs

1 yam

1 bunch asparagus

1 pint cherry tomatoes

1 bunch green onions

1-2 tablespoons avocado oil

Himalayan sea salt, to taste

METHOD

1. Preheat the oven to 350°F (180°C).

2. Heat up 1-2 tablespoons of avocado oil in an *oven-safe* fry pan over medium to medium-high heat. Crumble the sausage into the pan, breaking up the lumps. If your sausage is in casings, remove it from the casings using a knife or kitchen shears. Cook until the sausage is browned.

3. Remove the sausage from the pan with a slotted spoon, to keep the cooking fat from the sausage in the pan.

4. Prepare your veggies: peel and chop your yam into small cubes; break off the ends of the asparagus and chop into pieces similar in size to your yams; cut all of your cherry tomatoes in half; and cut off the root end of the green onions, and slice thinly.

5. Add the veggies to the cooking fat in your fry pan, and sauté until just tender. The yams will take the longest to cook, so add those first, and add salt to the pan with the yams and stir. After 1 minute add your asparagus, with salt, and stir. After another minute, add your tomatoes and onions, add salt, and stir all the veggies together.

6. Layer the veggies in the bottom of the pan, and add your cooked sausage on top of the veggies.

7. In a mixing bowl, whisk your raw eggs with salt and then pour them over the veggie/meat mixture.

8. Continue to cook on the stove-top for another 5 minutes to allow the frittata to set.

9. Place the frittata in the oven to finish cooking for 30-35 minutes.

VEGGIE-FRIED CAULIFLOWER RICE

Hands-On Time: 20 minutes
Cook Time: 30 minutes
Makes: 4-6 servings

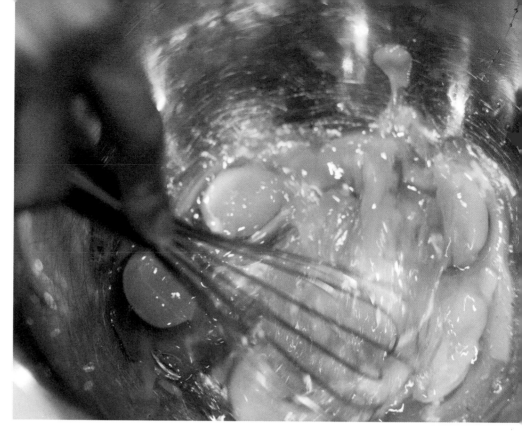

INGREDIENTS

1 package bacon

1 large or 2 small heads of cauliflower

6 eggs

Himalayan sea salt, to taste

2 tablespoons avocado oil

4 carrots

1 large or 2 small zucchini

½ pound (227g) mushrooms

1-inch square piece of fresh ginger (peeled and grated)

1 tablespoon garlic cloves (minced)

¼ cup (60ml) coconut aminos (recommend *Coconut Secrets*)

1 tablespoon coconut vinegar (recommend *Coconut Secrets*)

METHOD

1. Heat your Dutch oven over medium to medium-high heat. Using your kitchen shears, cut the slices of bacon directly into your Dutch oven: cut the pieces of bacon crosswise into ¼ to ½-inch pieces. Cook your bacon fully (to your preference), and remove from the Dutch oven using a slotted spoon, so that the bacon fat remains in the pot.

2. While the bacon is cooking, whisk your eggs with salt, in a mixing bowl. Once you've removed the bacon from your Dutch oven, add the whisked, raw eggs to the bacon fat, and cook up an omelet or scrambled eggs. Once the eggs are cooked, transfer to a cutting board and cut into small pieces. Set aside.

3. Prepare your veggies: peel and dice your carrots; dice your zucchinis to the same size as your carrot pieces; dice your mushrooms using the S-blade on your food processor.

4. Rice your cauliflower: remove the green leaves/stems, and cut out the core with your knife. Cut off any excess stems, and cut the cauliflower into evenly sized florets. Add your florets to the food processor in 1-2 batches, and "pulse" using your S-blade to create cauliflower pieces the size of rice grains.

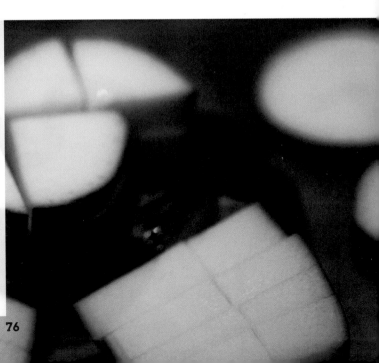

5. In your Dutch oven, heat up 1-2 tablespoons avocado oil over medium to medium-high heat. Add your carrots and season with salt, to taste. Cook your carrots, for 1-2 minutes, then add your zucchini, mushrooms, ginger (peel your ginger piece and grate directly into your Dutch oven) and minced garlic (using a garlic press) and add more salt, to taste. Add the lid and cook the veggies for several more minutes until all the vegetables have softened slightly.

6. Add your riced cauliflower to the Dutch oven, and season with salt.

7. Place the lid back on your Dutch oven and cook until the cauliflower is soft.

8. Once the veggies are cooked to your preferred tenderness, add in the eggs, bacon, coconut aminos, and coconut vinegar, and stir to combine.

PALEO FISH TACOS

Hands-On Time: 10 minutes
Cook Time: 15-20 minutes
Makes: 10 tacos

INGREDIENTS

Fish
1 pound (454g) of a white flaky fish (skin removed) such as cod, mahi-mahi, or tilapia

Himalayan sea salt, to taste

Cumin, to taste

Chili powder, to taste

Paprika, to taste

Garlic powder, to taste

Onion powder, to taste

Paleo Tortillas
1 ¾ cup (214g) *Otto's Naturals* Cassava Flour (order online)

½ cup plus **1** tablespoon and **1** teaspoon Avocado oil (134ml)

1 ¾ cup (412ml) filtered warm water

Pinch of Himalayan sea salt

Any Paleo toppings you like on your tacos, such as *Primal Kitchen* Chipotle Lime Mayo; pico de gallo or other favorite salsa; guacamole; cilantro; diced onion; diced tomatoes; sliced olives; shredded cabbage; lime juice.

METHOD

Fish

1. Preheat your oven to 375°F (190°C).
2. Cover a 12 x 17-inch baking sheet with parchment paper.
3. Place the fish pieces on the parchment paper.
4. Season the fish generously with salt, cumin, chili powder, paprika, garlic powder and onion powder.
5. Turn the fish over and season the other side with all of the same spices.
6. Bake for 7 minutes on the first side, then flip over the fish and bake another 7-10 minutes, depending on the thickness of the fish pieces.
7. Once the fish is finished cooking, break into small pieces.

Paleo Tortillas

1. In a large mixing bowl, whisk together the cassava flour and salt.
2. Add the warm water and oil and knead until the dough is smooth. The dough should not be too dry or too wet (add more flour, water and/or avocado oil as needed).
3. Divide the dough evenly into 10 balls, and place each ball between two pieces of parchment paper. Using your hands, the back of a spatula or a tortilla press, flatten each dough ball into the thickness of a tortilla.
4. Heat a dry skillet over medium-high heat, and then place the tortillas into the skillet in batches (1-2 at a time). Wait for air bubbles to form and then flip the tortillas, and cook the second side for 1-2 minutes.
5. Add your favorite Paleo toppings to create your Paleo Fish Tacos!

NOTES

Scale recipe down to make a smaller batch of 2 Paleo Tortillas:

¼ cup (30g) Otto's Naturals Cassava Flour

4 teaspoons avocado oil

¼ cup (56ml) filtered warm water

Pinch of Himalayan sea salt

Paleo Tortillas
These are great, healthy carbs for adding to meals like breakfast tacos, or spiced ground beef tacos (see week #4). You can also add some ghee and cinnamon to the tortillas for a sweet treat. Pre-make your tortillas by making a large batch of the dough, and layering parchment paper between each tortilla before storing in the fridge.

Paleo Fish Tacos
If you don't have any pre-made tortillas, nor the time to make some, just make a taco salad with the fish, and all the taco toppings. Don't forget the Primal Kitchen Chipotle Lime Mayonnaise.

CAULIFLOWER BUFFALO WINGS

Hands-On Time: 20 minutes   **Cook Time**: 30-35 minutes   **Makes**: 4-6 servings

METHOD

1. Preheat the oven to 425°F (220°C).

2. Prepare your cauliflower: remove the green leaves/stems, and cut out the core with your knife. Cut off any excess stems, and cut the cauliflower into small, bite-size florets.

3. Add your cauliflower florets to a large mixing bowl.

4. In a separate, medium-size mixing bowl, combine your almond flour, salt, paprika and garlic powder.

5. In another smaller, mixing bowl, combine your avocado oil and hot sauce. Pour the oil/hot sauce over the cauliflower florets and stir together until all florets are well coated.

6. Then pour the spiced almond flour mixture over the florets, and stir until all of the florets are coated with the spiced almond flour.

7. Cover a rimmed 12 x 17-inch baking sheet with parchment paper.

8. Pour the florets from the mixing bowl onto the baking sheet, and spread them out so that they are not overlapping.

9. Bake for 30-35 minutes or until the florets are a little crispy.

INGREDIENTS

1 large or 2 small heads of cauliflower

1 cup (100g) almond flour

1 teaspoon Himalayan sea salt

1 teaspoon smoked paprika

1 teaspoon garlic powder

¼ cup (56ml) avocado oil

1 teaspoon hot sauce (use whole, natural ingredients and spices)

Parchment paper

WEEK #4

MEALS + SNACKS:

- ▶ Paleo Quiche
- ▶ Paleo Pumpkin Muffins
- ▶ Tuna Salad with Bacon-Wrapped Green Beans
- ▶ Spiced Ground Beef with Mexican Cauli-Rice

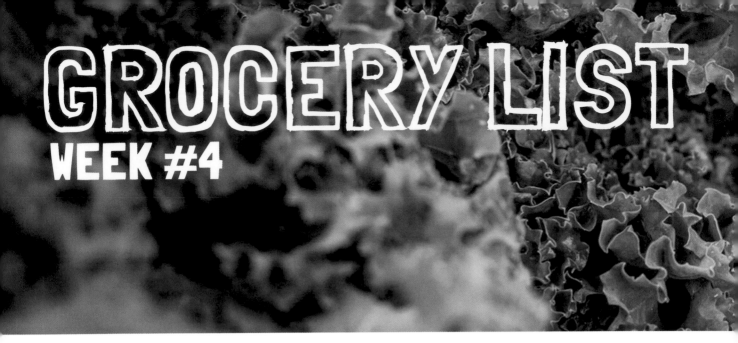

GROCERY LIST
WEEK #4

Recommendations: buy organic and locally grown produce; buy organic, pasture-raised meat, poultry and eggs; and buy wild-caught fish, whenever possible.

PRODUCE

- Cauliflower (1 large or 2 small heads)
- Yellow onion (1)
- Bell peppers (2; any color)
- Carrots (4)
- Fresh chilies (1-2, mild to medium flavor)
- Fresh cilantro (½ cup/25g, chopped)
- Garlic cloves (2 tablespoons, minced)
- Shallot (2 large)
- Green beans (½ pound/227g)
- Baby spinach (5 ounces/142g)

MEAT + POULTRY + FISH + EGGS

- 10 eggs
- 2 packages bacon
- 1 pound/454g ground beef
- 3 tablespoons butter

NUTS + SEEDS + OILS

- Avocado oil (1½ cups/355ml)
- Almond flour (3¾ cups/360g)
- Walnuts (¼ cup/33g, chopped)

SPICES

- Himalayan sea salt (2 tablespoons plus ½ teaspoon, and more to taste)
- Ground mustard (½ teaspoon)
- Ground cinnamon (1 teaspoon)
- Ground nutmeg (⅛ teaspoon)
- Ground cloves (a pinch)
- Baking soda (¼ teaspoon)
- Chili powder (1 tablespoon)
- Ground cumin (2 teaspoons)
- Garlic granules (2 teaspoons)
- Paprika (1 teaspoon)
- Ground black pepper (½ teaspoon)

CANNED + JARRED + PACKAGED GOODS

- Lime juice (2 tablespoons)
- Lemon juice (¼ cup/59ml)
- Tomato paste (2 tablespoons)
- Fire-roasted diced tomatoes (one 14.5-ounce/429ml can)
- Wild albacore canned tuna (four 5-ounce/142g cans; recommend *Wild Planet*)
- Yellow mustard (2 tablespoons; use whole, natural ingredients and spices)
- 1 Paleo dill pickle (use whole, natural ingredients and spices - no sugar or additives)
- Pumpkin puree (¾ cup/170g)
- Maple syrup (½ cup/175g)
- Raisins (¼ cup/40g)
- *Otto's Naturals* Cassava Flour (2 tablespoons)
- *Primal Kitchen* Mayo (2 tablespoons)

COOKING SUPPLIES

- Parchment paper
- Parchment paper muffin liners (one dozen)

COOKING ORDER WEEK #4:

1. Preheat the oven to 325°F (165°C).
2. Make <u>Paleo Quiche</u>.
3. Turn up the oven to 350°F (180°C).
4. Make <u>Paleo Pumpkin Muffins</u>.
5. Make <u>Tuna Salad</u>.
6. Turn up the oven to 400°F (200°C).
7. Make <u>Bacon-Wrapped Green Beans</u>.
8. Make <u>Mexican Cauli-Rice</u>.
9. Make <u>Spiced Ground Beef</u>.

PALEO QUICHE

Hands-On Time: 25 minutes
Cook Time: 30-35 minutes
Makes: 6-8 servings

INGREDIENTS

2 ½ cups (240g) almond flour

2 tablespoons *Otto's Naturals* Cassava Flour

½ teaspoon Himalayan sea salt (plus more to taste)

3 tablespoons cold butter

7 eggs

2 tablespoons filtered iced water

1 package bacon

5 ounces (142g) baby spinach

1 large shallot

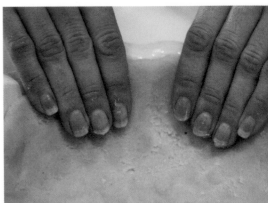
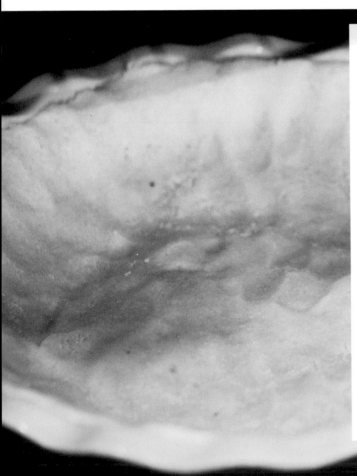

METHOD

1. Preheat the oven to 325°F (165°C).

2. Add almond flour, cassava flour, and salt (½ teaspoon) to your food processor, and pulse to combine.

3. Cut your cold butter into small cubes, and add the butter pieces to your food processor. Process until all of the butter is mixed in.

4. Add one egg and your cold, filtered water to the food processor, and process until a dough ball is formed.

5. Put the dough ball into the bottom of a pie pan, and spread out the dough until you form a quiche crust along the bottom and sides.

6. Put the plain crust in the oven and bake for 10 minutes.

7. Dice your shallot and set aside.

8. Heat up a skillet over medium to medium-high heat. Using your kitchen shears, cut the slices of bacon directly into your skillet: cut the pieces of bacon crosswise into ¼ to ½-inch pieces. When the bacon is almost done cooking, add your diced shallots, spinach, and salt, to taste. Continue cooking until the bacon is cooked as you like it.

9. Remove your quiche crust from the oven and add the bacon/spinach/shallot mixture to the bottom of the crust.

10. Whisk six eggs with salt, to taste, in a mixing bowl and pour the whisked, raw eggs over the top of the bacon mixture.

11. Bake for 30-35 minutes.

NOTES

This recipe is a consistent favorite among my clients and is both freezable and a great template recipe - easy to substitute in your favorite ingredients.

PALEO PUMPKIN MUFFINS

Hands-On Time: 15 minutes **Cook Time**: 30-35 minutes **Makes**: 12 muffins

INGREDIENTS

1 ¼ cups (120g) almond flour

¼ teaspoon baking soda

½ teaspoon Himalayan sea salt

1 teaspoon ground cinnamon

⅛ teaspoon ground nutmeg

Pinch of ground cloves

¾ cup (170g) pumpkin puree

2 eggs

½ cup (175g) maple syrup

¼ cup (30g) chopped walnuts

¼ cup (40g) raisins

1 dozen parchment paper muffin liners

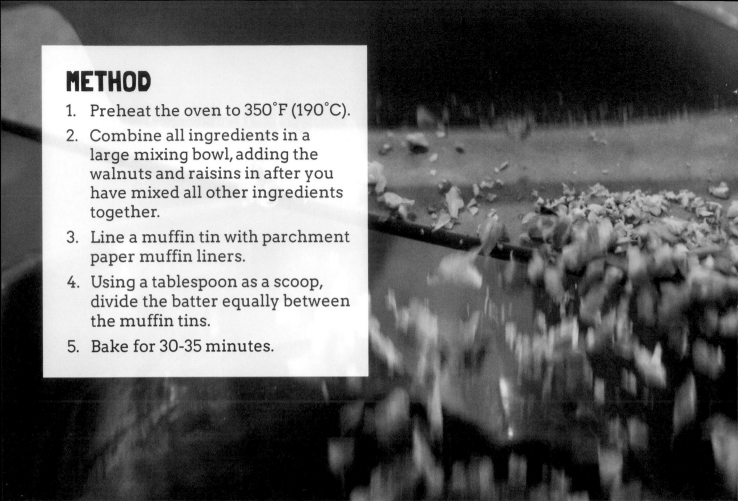

METHOD

1. Preheat the oven to 350°F (190°C).

2. Combine all ingredients in a large mixing bowl, adding the walnuts and raisins in after you have mixed all other ingredients together.

3. Line a muffin tin with parchment paper muffin liners.

4. Using a tablespoon as a scoop, divide the batter equally between the muffin tins.

5. Bake for 30-35 minutes.

TUNA SALAD

INGREDIENTS

Paleo Mayonnaise

1 egg

2 tablespoons lemon juice

1¼ cups (296ml) avocado oil

½ teaspoon ground mustard

½ teaspoon Himalayan sea salt

Or you can use ¼ cup (60g) plus
1 tablespoon of *Primal Kitchen* Mayo
(sold in stores and online)

Tuna Salad

4 (5-ounce/142g) cans wild albacore
canned tuna (recommend *Wild
Planet)*

2 tablespoons yellow mustard
(use whole, natural ingredients
and spices)

2 tablespoons shallot (minced)

2 tablespoons lemon juice

1 Paleo dill pickle (use whole, natural
ingredients and spices - no sugar or
additives)

½ teaspoon Himalayan sea salt

METHOD

1. <u>Make your Paleo Mayonnaise:</u> In a food processor, using an S-blade, combine the egg, lemon juice, mustard, salt and ¼ cup of the avocado oil. While the food processor is running, *slowly* drizzle in the remaining 1 cup of oil. This should take 2-3 minutes to finish making the mayonnaise.

2. Dice your shallot until you have 2 tablespoons.

3. Dice your pickle.

4. Add all of the ingredients and tuna to a large mixing bowl and stir with a fork to combine.

Hands-On Time: 10 minutes **Cook Time**: 20-25 minutes **Makes**: 10-12 bundles

BACON-WRAPPED GREEN BEANS

NOTES

I eat these for breakfast!

INGREDIENTS

½ pound (227g) of green beans
1 package (10-12 slices) of bacon
Parchment paper

METHOD

1. Preheat the oven to 400°F (200°C).
2. Cover a large rimmed (12 x 17-inch) baking sheet with parchment paper.
3. Trim off the ends of your green beans.
4. Wrap 4-6 green beans in a piece of uncooked bacon and lay each bundle on the baking sheet. You should have enough green beans for 10-12 bundles, depending on how much bacon you use.
5. Cook for 20-25 minutes.
6. Save the remaining bacon fat in a jar and store in the fridge to use as cooking oil!

Hands-On Time: 25 minutes **Cook Time**: 15 minutes **Makes**: 4-6 servings

MEXICAN
CAULI-RICE

INGREDIENTS

1-2 tablespoons avocado oil

1 teaspoon Himalayan sea salt (plus more to taste)

4 carrots

1 yellow onion

2 bell peppers (any color)

1-2 fresh chilies (mild to medium flavor)

1 large or 2 small heads of cauliflower

2 tablespoons garlic cloves (minced)

½ cup (25g) fresh cilantro (chopped)

2 tablespoons tomato paste

1 (14.5-ounce/411g) can fire-roasted diced tomatoes

2 tablespoons lime juice

METHOD

1. Prepare your veggies: peel your carrots and yellow onion, then dice them along with your bell peppers and chilies into small pieces.

2. Rice your cauliflower: remove the green leaves/stems, and remove the core with your knife. Cut off any excess stems, and cut the cauliflower into evenly-sized florets. Add your florets to the food processor in 1-2 batches, and "pulse" using your S-blade to create cauliflower pieces the size of rice grains.

3. In your Dutch oven, heat up 1-2 tablespoons avocado oil over medium to medium-high heat. Add your onions, peppers, carrots, chilies, cauliflower and minced garlic (using a garlic press) to your Dutch oven, and season with salt, to taste. Add the lid to your Dutch oven and cook until all the vegetables have softened slightly, about 5 minutes.

4. While the vegetables are cooking, remove the cilantro leaves from the stems and finely chop up ½ cup of cilantro leaves.

5. Remove the lid, and add your diced tomatoes (with the juice), tomato paste, and salt. Cook for about another 5-7 minutes with the lid on or until all of the vegetables have cooked to your preference.

6. Once all the veggies are fully cooked, add in the lime juice and cilantro, stirring to combine. Add additional salt, if preferred.

SPICED GROUND BEEF

Hands-On Time: 15 minutes
Cook Time: 10 minutes
Makes: 4-6 servings

INGREDIENTS

1 pound (454g) ground beef

1 tablespoon chili powder

2 teaspoons ground cumin

2 teaspoons garlic granules

1 teaspoon paprika

2 teaspoons Himalayan sea salt

½ teaspoon ground black pepper

1-2 tablespoons avocado oil

METHOD

1. Add all of your spices to a small bowl, and stir to combine.

2. Add your ground beef to a separate mixing bowl, and pour your spice rub into the bowl with the beef. Use your hands to mix the spice rub into the ground beef.

3. Heat 1-2 tablespoons of avocado oil in your skillet over medium heat.

4. Add your spiced ground beef to the hot skillet, and cook until the meat is browned.

NOTES

*Make Paleo Ground Beef Tacos! Follow the tortilla recipe on page 79 (**Paleo Fish Tacos**) and add your favorite Paleo taco toppings: Primal Kitchen Chipotle Lime Mayo; pico de gallo or other favorite salsa; guacamole; cilantro; diced onion; diced tomatoes; sliced olives; shredded lettuce; diced tomatoes, etc.*

GROCERY + COOKING ORDER CHECKLISTS

Photocopy these pages and take them with you when you go shopping.

Each week's Grocery List is on the front, with the Cooking Order on the back.

GROCERY LIST: WEEK #1

Recommendations: buy organic and locally grown produce; buy organic, pasture-raised meat, poultry and eggs and wild-caught fish whenever possible.

PRODUCE
- ❏ Spaghetti squash (2 to 3 pounds/1-1.36kg, or if not available, 2 yams, spiralized)
- ❏ Yams (2)
- ❏ Baby spinach (5 ounces/142g)
- ❏ Collard greens (12 large leaves)
- ❏ Any veggies you like on your sandwiches (ie; 2-3 tomatoes, or 1 red onion, etc.)
- ❏ Yellow onion (1)
- ❏ Carrots (9)
- ❏ Cherry tomatoes (1 pint)
- ❏ Cucumbers (1-2; for Raw Veggie Snack Bags)
- ❏ Butternut squash (1 small; or if not available, 2 yams)
- ❏ Garlic cloves (2 cloves and 2 tablespoons, minced)
- ❏ Mushrooms (½ pound/227g, sliced)
- ❏ Cauliflower (1 head)

MEAT + POULTRY + FISH + EGGS
- ❏ 1½ dozen eggs
- ❏ 1 pound/454g mild Italian pork sausage
- ❏ 12 slices of lunch meat (if using 2 slices per sandwich wrap)
- ❏ 2 packages of bacon
- ❏ 1 pound/454g ground beef
- ❏ 1 pound/454g ground pork

NUTS + SEEDS + OILS
- ❏ Avocado oil (¼ cup/56ml and 2 tablespoons, plus more to coat baking dish)
- ❏ Extra virgin olive oil (EVOO) (½ cup/112ml)

- ❏ Tahini (⅓ cup/79ml)
- ❏ Almond butter (½ cup/113g - the only ingredients should be almonds, and salt or no salt)
- ❏ Go Raw Organic, Sprouted Sunflower Seeds (½ cup/58g)
- ❏ Unsweetened, shredded coconut (½ cup/50g)

SPICES
- ❏ Vanilla extract (1 teaspoon)
- ❏ Cinnamon (1 teaspoon)
- ❏ Baking soda (¼ teaspoon)
- ❏ Himalayan sea salt (1¼ teaspoon, plus more to taste)
- ❏ Cumin (½ teaspoon)

CANNED + JARRED + PACKAGED GOODS
- ❏ Maple syrup (½ cup/175g)
- ❏ Cacao nibs (½ cup/58g)
- ❏ Any *Paleo* condiments you like on your sandwiches (*Primal Kitchen* Mayo, mustard, Paleo pickles, etc.)
- ❏ Tomato paste (6-ounce/180ml can)
- ❏ *Cucina Antica* Garlic Marinara sauce (one 32-ounce/904g jar)
- ❏ Lemon juice (⅓ cup/79g)

COOKING SUPPLIES
- ❏ Parchment paper muffin liners (one dozen)
- ❏ Aluminum foil
- ❏ Parchment paper
- ❏ Sandwich-size plastic bags (5)

COOKING ORDER: WEEK #1

1. Preheat the oven to 350°F (180°C).
2. Make **Paleo Energy Muffins**.
3. Turn up the oven to 400°F (200°C).
4. Make **Roasted Spaghetti Squash**.
5. Make the **Breakfast Casserole**.
6. Put the casserole in the oven with the **Roasted Spaghetti Squash**.
7. Make **Paleo Winter Ragu**. Simmer for 1 hour.
8. Turn up the oven to 425°F (220°C).
9. Make the bacon for the **Paleo Collard Greens Sandwich Wraps**.
10. Roast cauliflower for **Paleo Hummus**.
11. Put the cauliflower in the oven with the bacon.
12. Make **Paleo Collard Greens Sandwich Wraps** (*recommendation*: do not pre-make all sandwich wraps; it's best to make them throughout the week, on the day of or night before).
13. Make **Raw Veggie Snack Bags**.
14. Make **Paleo Hummus**.

GROCERY LIST: WEEK #2

Recommendations: buy organic and locally grown produce; buy organic, pasture-raised meat, poultry and eggs and wild-caught fish whenever possible.

PRODUCE
- ☐ Cherry tomatoes (1 pint)
- ☐ Carrots (6)
- ☐ Cucumbers (2)
- ☐ Green onions (1 bunch)
- ☐ Radishes (1 bunch)
- ☐ Beet (1)
- ☐ Spinach (5 ounces/142g) or Romaine lettuce (1 bunch)
- ☐ Garlic cloves (1 teaspoon, minced)
- ☐ Sun-dried tomatoes (2 ounces/57g)
- ☐ Leek (1)
- ☐ Mushrooms (1 pound/454g)
- ☐ Bananas (4, very ripe)
- ☐ Bell peppers (4, any color)
- ☐ Yellow onion (1)

MEAT + POULTRY + FISH + EGG
- ☐ 3 pounds/1.36kg pork shoulder/butt (ask the butcher to cut into two 1½-pound/680g pieces)
- ☐ 3 pounds/1.36kg boneless, chicken thighs (or any other preferred type of chicken)
- ☐ 1 pound/454g mild Italian pork sausage
- ☐ 14 eggs

NUTS + SEEDS + OILS
- ☐ Extra virgin olive oil (EVOO) (½ cup/112ml)
- ☐ Avocado oil (¾ cup/177ml)
- ☐ Unrefined coconut oil (¼ cup/56ml)
- ☐ Almond flour (2 cups/280g)
- ☐ Walnuts (½ cup/65g, chopped)

SPICES
- ☐ Smoked paprika (6 tablespoons, plus more to taste)
- ☐ Garlic cloves (1 teaspoon, minced)
- ☐ Garlic granules, to taste
- ☐ Garlic powder (2 tablespoons)
- ☐ Ground mustard (2 tablespoons, plus more to taste)
- ☐ Himalayan sea salt (3 tablespoons and ¾ teaspoon, plus more to taste)
- ☐ Ground black pepper (¼ teaspoon)
- ☐ Vanilla extract (1 teaspoon)
- ☐ Baking soda (½ teaspoon)

CANNED + JARRED + PACKAGED GOODS
- ☐ Dijon mustard (1 teaspoon)
- ☐ Balsamic vinegar (3 tablespoons)
- ☐ Maple syrup (¼ cup/56ml)

COOKING SUPPLIES
- ☐ Parchment paper
- ☐ Parchment paper muffin liners (2 dozen)

COOKING ORDER: WEEK #2

1. ***The night before:*** Make the spice rub for the **Carnitas** and marinate the meat in the fridge **overnight**.

2. ***The morning of:*** Put the Carnitas in the slow cooker as soon as you wake up in the morning, since they will need to cook for 8 hours on low.

3. Preheat the oven to 350°F (180°C).

4. Make the **Paleo Banana Nut Muffins**.

5. Turn up the oven to 375°F (190°C).

6. Make the **Paleo Egg Muffins**.

7. Turn up the oven to 400°F (200°C).

8. Make **Roasted Chicken**.

9. Make **Fajita Veggies** (Just pre-cut the veggies, and cook up one serving; store the rest of the pre-cut veggies in the fridge and cook up a serving the day of or the night before).

10. Make **Mason Jar Salads**.

11. Make **Simple Vinaigrette**.

GROCERY LIST: WEEK #3

Recommendations: buy organic and locally grown produce; buy organic, pasture-raised meat, poultry and eggs and wild-caught fish whenever possible.

PRODUCE

- ☐ Garlic cloves (4 cloves and 1 tablespoon, minced)
- ☐ Cauliflower (2 large heads or 4 small)
- ☐ Carrots (4)
- ☐ Zucchini (1 large or 2 small)
- ☐ Mushrooms (½ pound/227g)
- ☐ Fresh ginger (1-inch square piece)
- ☐ Yam (1)
- ☐ Asparagus (1 bunch)
- ☐ Cherry tomatoes (1 pint)
- ☐ Green onions (1 bunch)
- ☐ Any veggies you like on your Paleo Fish Tacos (pico de gallo or other favorite salsa; guacamole; cilantro; diced onion; shredded cabbage; lime juice, etc.)

MEAT + POULTRY + FISH + EGGS

- ☐ 1½ pounds/681g flank steak (ask the butcher to cut the steak into six 4-ounce/113.5g pieces)
- ☐ 1 package bacon
- ☐ 18 eggs
- ☐ 1 pound/454g mild Italian, pork sausage
- ☐ 1 pound/454g of a white flaky fish (skin removed) such as cod, mahi mahi, or tilapia

NUTS + SEEDS + OILS

- ☐ Avocado oil (1⅓ cup and 4 teaspoons/335ml, plus more to fry the steaks)
- ☐ Coconut aminos (⅓ cup plus ¼ cup/135ml; recommend *Coconut Secrets*)
- ☐ Coconut vinegar (1 tablespoon; recommend *Coconut Secrets*)
- ☐ Unsweetened coconut flakes (1 cup/115g)

- ☐ Unrefined/extra virgin coconut oil (¼ cup/50g)
- ☐ Almond flour (1 cup/115g)
- ☐ Raw almonds (1 cup/115g)
- ☐ Raw cashews (1 cup/115g)
- ☐ Raw pumpkin seeds (1 cup/115g)
- ☐ Raw sunflower seeds (1 cup/115g)

SPICES

- ☐ Himalayan sea salt (2¼ teaspoons, plus more to taste)
- ☐ Smoked paprika (1 teaspoon)
- ☐ Garlic powder (1 teaspoon, plus more to taste)
- ☐ Vanilla extract (1 teaspoon)
- ☐ Cumin, to taste
- ☐ Chili powder, to taste
- ☐ Paprika, to taste
- ☐ Onion powder, to taste

CANNED + JARRED + PACKAGED GOODS

- ☐ Apple cider vinegar (1 tablespoon)
- ☐ Hot sauce (1 teaspoon; only whole, natural ingredients and spices)
- ☐ Raw honey (½ cup/88g)
- ☐ Cacao nibs (1 cup/115g)
- ☐ *Primal Kitchen* Chipotle Lime Mayo as a condiment for your Paleo Fish Tacos

COOKING SUPPLIES

- ☐ Parchment paper

ONLINE

- ☐ *Otto's Naturals* Cassava Flour (1¾ cup/214g)

COOKING ORDER: WEEK #3

1. ***The night before*** make the marinade for the **Paleo Honey Garlic Flank Steak** and ***marinate the meat*** in the fridge ***overnight***.

2. Preheat the oven to 350°F (180°C).

3. Make the **Paleo Granola**.

4. Make the **Paleo Frittata**.

5. Make the **Veggie-Fried Cauliflower Rice**.

6. Turn up the oven to 375°F (190°C).

7. Make the fish for the **Paleo Fish Tacos**.

8. Turn up the oven to 425°F (220°C).

9. Make **Cauliflower Buffalo Wings**.

10. Make the tortillas for the **Paleo Fish Tacos**.

GROCERY LIST: WEEK #4

Recommendations: buy organic and locally grown produce; buy organic, pasture-raised meat, poultry and eggs and wild-caught fish whenever possible.

PRODUCE

- ❑ Cauliflower (1 large or 2 small heads)
- ❑ Yellow onion (1)
- ❑ Bell peppers (2; any color)
- ❑ Carrots (4)
- ❑ Fresh chilies (1-2, mild to medium flavor)
- ❑ Fresh cilantro (½ cup/25g, chopped)
- ❑ Garlic cloves (2 tablespoons, minced)
- ❑ Shallot (2 large)
- ❑ Green beans (½ pound/227g)
- ❑ Baby spinach (5 ounces/142g)

MEAT + POULTRY + FISH + EGGS

- ❑ 10 eggs
- ❑ 2 packages bacon
- ❑ 1 pound/454g ground beef
- ❑ 3 tablespoons butter

NUTS + SEEDS + OILS

- ❑ Avocado oil (1½ cups/355ml)
- ❑ Almond flour (3¾ cups/360g)
- ❑ Walnuts (¼ cup, chopped/33g)

SPICES

- ❑ Himalayan sea salt (2 tablespoons and ½ teaspoon, plus more to taste)
- ❑ Ground mustard (½ teaspoon)
- ❑ Ground cinnamon (1 teaspoon)
- ❑ Ground nutmeg (⅛ teaspoon)
- ❑ Ground cloves (a pinch)
- ❑ Baking soda (¼ teaspoon)
- ❑ Chili powder (1 tablespoon)
- ❑ Ground cumin (2 teaspoons)
- ❑ Garlic granules (2 teaspoons)
- ❑ Paprika (1 teaspoon)
- ❑ Ground black pepper (½ teaspoon)

CANNED + JARRED + PACKAGED GOODS

- ❑ Lime juice (2 tablespoons)
- ❑ Lemon juice (¼ cup/59ml)
- ❑ Tomato paste (2 tablespoons)
- ❑ Fire-roasted diced tomatoes (one 14.5-ounce/429ml can)
- ❑ Wild albacore canned tuna (four 5-ounce/142g cans; recommend *Wild Planet*)
- ❑ Yellow mustard (2 tablespoons; use whole, natural ingredients and spices)
- ❑ Paleo dill pickles (1; use whole, natural ingredients and spices - no sugar or additives!)
- ❑ Pumpkin puree (¾ cup/170g)
- ❑ Maple syrup (½ cup/175g)
- ❑ Raisins (¼ cup/40g)
- ❑ *Otto's Naturals* Cassava Flour (2 tablespoons)
- ❑ *Primal Kitchen* Mayo (2 tablespoons)

COOKING SUPPLIES

- ❑ Parchment paper
- ❑ Parchment paper muffin liners (one dozen)

COOKING ORDER: WEEK #4

1. Preheat the oven to 325°F (165°C).
2. Make **Paleo Quiche**.
3. Turn up the oven to 350°F (180°C).
4. Make **Paleo Pumpkin Muffins**.
5. Make **Tuna Salad**.
6. Turn up the oven to 400°F (200°C).
7. Make **Bacon-Wrapped Green Beans**.
8. Make **Mexican Cauli-Rice**.
9. Make **Spiced Ground Beef**.

INDEX